Birth and Baptism Records for Family Historians

Stuart A. Raymond

VITAL
RECORDS
FOR FAMILY
HISTORIANS
1

THE FAMILY HISTORY PARTNERSHIP

Published by
The Family History Partnership
PO Box 502
Bury, Lancashire BL8 9EP
Webpage: www.familyhistorypartnership.co.uk
Email: sales@thefamilyhistorypartnership.com

in association with
S.A. & M.J. Raymond
Webpage: www.stuartraymond.co.uk
Email: samjraymond@btopenworld.com

ISBNs:
Family History Partnership: 978 1 906280 24 6
S.A. & M.J. Raymond: 978 1 899668 54 0

First Published 2010

Cover illustration:
from *Punch,* vol. 1, 1841, p.171

Printed and bound by
Information Press. Southfield Road, Eynsham
Oxford OX29 4JB

Contents

1. Introduction

Who were your parents and grandparents? And who were their parents and grandparents? It is impossible to construct your family tree without answers to these questions. Fortunately, in England and Wales, births and/or baptisms have been registered for almost 500 years. Parentage has usually been recorded in these registers, together with either the date of birth or the date of baptism - sometimes both. Civil registers of births have been maintained since 1837. Baptisms have been recorded in parish registers since 1538. Most registers from the eighteenth century and later have survived. Earlier registers have not fared as well, but many are still available.

A variety of other registers are also available. Registers were kept by non-conformists, by Huguenots, and by Roman Catholics. Baptisms could take place in garrisons, in overseas embassies, on ships, in schools, and in hospitals. The masters of workhouses had to keep registers of births.

In addition to formal registers, a variety of other sources provide clues which can help you to trace births. Census returns give the ages of individuals, and (from 1851) their birthplaces. Manorial court rolls and inquisitions post mortem both give details of heirs. Wills identify the surviving children of the deceased, sometimes giving their ages. Occupational sources, such as apprenticeship indentures, frequently give ages, parentage, and birthplaces. Deeds and leases may help you to identify parents and their children.

2. Civil Registers

If you are trying to construct a pedigree for a family who lived in England and Wales after 1837, then you will need to consult the civil registers. These give the details of births which you will need in order to prove the parentage of your ancestors. The registers themselves are not open to public inspection. To find information in them, you must consult the indexes. These are widely available, and an initial search may be straightforward. There are, however, potential pitfalls. You need to be aware of these. You also need to be aware that there are a variety of approaches to using these registers. It is important to understand how they have been compiled.

The civil registration of births in England and Wales commenced on 1st July 1837, in accordance with the Births & Deaths Registration Act 1836. Initially, the responsibility for registering births lay with local Registrars, who were expected to monitor all births within their districts, and to register them within 42 days. No responsibility was placed upon families to report births, although families were required to answer registrars' questions.

The illiterate in nineteenth-century England could not read public notices, and may have been unaware of the requirement for civil registration. Some continued to assume that baptism in the Church was all that was necessary. There was no provision for the clergy to report baptisms to registrars. The opposition of some clergy to compulsory registration did not help. And the introduction of compulsory vaccination for smallpox in 1853[1] led some parents to avoid registration if possible. It has been estimated that, prior to the Births & Deaths Registration Act 1874, up to 15% of all births may have gone unrecorded in the civil registers. Sometimes, it may be necessary to search other records (see below) for births in this period.

The Births and Deaths Registration Act 1874 placed the onus for reporting births and deaths on parents and families, and prescribed penalties for failing to do so. Late registration incurred a penalty, which caused some parents to report a later date of birth than was actually the case. The 1874 Act also tightened up procedures for registering illegitimate children. Hitherto, information about their paternity had been supplied solely by the mother. Sometimes the latter gave false information. Henceforth, fathers' names were only registered if the father accompanied the mother to register the child.

Non-registration was considerably reduced by this act, but it was not almost completely eliminated until the twentieth century. Some parents continued to avoid registration until compulsory vaccination was abolished in 1898. But the spread of literacy, the fall in the number of home births, and the fact that bureaucrats frequently required the production of birth certificates, meant that it became increasingly important to register, and increasingly difficult to avoid registration.

A number of changes to the system took place in 1926 and 1927. The Legitimacy Act 1926 made provision for the births of illegitimate children to be reregistered on the marriage of their parents, in order to give them legitimacy. From 1927, all still-births had to be registered.

The civil registers of births were and are compiled by district registrars under the supervision of superintendant registrars. These registers are still held by district registrars, unless they have been deposited in local record offices. For details of district registrars, see:

+ Registration Districts of England and Wales (1837-1974)
  www.ukbmd.org.uk/genuki/reg
+ LANGSTON, BRETT. *A handbook to the civil registration districts of England and Wales*. The Author, 2001.
+ WIGGINS, RAY. *Registration districts: an alphabetical list of over 650 districts with details of counties, sub-districts and adjacent districts*. 3rd ed. Society of Genealogists Enterprises, 2003.
+ Direct Gov: Search for your Local Register Office
  http://maps.direct.gov.uk/LDGRedirect/MapAction.do?ref=grolight

---

[1] It is worth noting that, from 1871, registrars were required to send a return of all births, and deaths of children under 12 months, to their local Medical Officer of Health. Such notifications may still survive in local record offices.

Each quarter, the district registers were copied in order to compile a return for the Registrar General. His staff then copied the copy in order to compile the General Register Office (GRO) registers. The latter are therefore copies of copies. Such copies are not error free. Nevertheless, they are the basis for the GRO's indexes, which were compiled quarterly for every year between 1837 and 1984. Since then, they have been compiled annually, by computer.

There are so many errors in the old indexes that an entirely new index is in preparation. Until that is complete - which could be some years - reliance must be placed on the original indexes.

That is unfortunate, since it is only through the civil registration indexes that access can be had to the information in the actual registers. The registers themselves are not open to public inspection. Instead, it is necessary to identify births through the indexes, and to apply for certificates setting out the information found in the registers. The use of the old indexes is therefore described below. There are a number of alternatives to using them, which will also be described. When the new index becomes available, the old ones will be superseded. You should therefore regularly check the GRO website **www.gro.gov.uk/gro/content/ aboutus/index.asp** for information on the current status of the new index.

The old indexes are widely available on the internet. A new database of the old index is currently being compiled by volunteers at FreeBMD **www.freebmd. org.uk.** This site is free, and should therefore be checked before you use any of the commercial sites. In contrast to most of the latter, it also takes you directly to the information you require. You do not need to read digitised images of the printed indexes, although these are available if you wish to check your information. Free BMD is almost complete for the nineteenth century, but so far there are few entries for the mid-1930s and later. The extent of its coverage can be viewed at **www.freebmd.org.uk/ progressB.shtml**.

If Free BMD does not cover the period you are interested in, there are a number of alternatives. The GRO registers are available on a number of commercial websites, and also on microform in many libraries. Commercial websites include:

+ 192.com
  www.192.com/Genealogy
+ Ancestry
  www.ancestry.co.uk
+ BMD Index
  www.bmdindex.co.uk
+ Family Relatives
  www.familyrelatives.com
+ Find My Past
  www.findmypast.com/BirthsMarriagesDeaths.jsp
+ The Genealogist
  www.thegenealogist.co.uk

- Genes Reunited
  www.genesreunited.co.uk/records

The GRO indexes can also be consulted on microform in many libraries and record offices. For a full list of these institutions, consult:
- Holders of the GRO Indexes
  www.gro.gov.uk/gro/content/research/groindexes/
  holders_of_the_gro_indexes.asp

The old indexes, as already noted, were compiled quarterly. Each quarterly index covers the births registered in that quarter. Many births were registered in the quarter which followed the quarter in which the birth took place, so you may need to check two quarterly indexes in order to find a particular birth.

The indexes give the basic information needed to purchase a birth certificate. That includes the name, the year of registration, the volume number, and the page number. Since the September quarter 1911, birth indexes have indicated mothers' maiden names. This may help to identify entries for people with names such as John Smith. It may also help to identify brothers and sisters without the need to spend money on certificates.

In a few instances, only the surname, together with the sex of the child, is given in the indexes. This occurred when the parents had not decided on a name at the time of registration, or when a baby died without having been baptised.

A very few entries in the birth indexes record children whose surnames had not been reported. Most of these - but not necessarily all - were foundling children. These entries can be found at the end of each index, after the entries for surnames beginning with 'Z'.

Once you have identified an index entry, you can place an order for a certificate. It is possible to do this online at **www.gro.gov.uk/gro/content/order_certificates/index.asp**. Certificates may also be applied for by post from the General Register Office, PO Box 2, Southport, Merseyside, PR8 2JD.

Do not be misled into applying for a short birth certificate. These are intended for administrative purposes such as obtaining a passport. They are useless for genealogical purposes, since they do not state parentage.

Birth certificates can also be obtained from district registrars, who maintain their own - quite separate - indexes. These indexes cannot be used to obtain certificates from the GRO, nor can GRO indexes be used to obtain certificates from district registrars. District registrars will search their indexes for you for a fee. Some will allow you to search them yourself, but again a fee is likely to be demanded. Arrangements for searching indexes vary between registrars.

An increasing number of indexes to district registers are available on the internet. These are likely to be more reliable than the GRO indexes, since they rely on the original registers rather than copies of copies of them. A gateway to these indexes is provided by:

* UKBMD
  www.ukbmd.org.uk
  (click `local bmd')

With the minor exceptions already noted, the basic information recorded in civil birth registers has been virtually constant since 1837. When you obtain a birth certificate, you can expect it to be headed with the registration district, sub-district, year of registration, and the number of the entry in the register. It will have 10 columns, headed:

1. When and where born
2. Name if any
3. Sex
4. Name and surname of father
5. Name, surname and maiden surname of mother
6. Occupation of father
7. Signature, description, and residence of informant
8. When registered
9. Signature of registrar
10. Name entered after registration

The surname of the child is not given. It was officially assumed to be that of the father, unless the child was illegitimate. A time against the date of birth may indicate twins. The eldest twin had to be identified, in order to settle any question of inheritance.

The term 'if any' in the column headed 'name if any' printed on certificates refers to the situation which arose when a baby had not been named before it was registered. Sometimes, these entries are for babies who died before they could be baptised. It may therefore be worth checking subsequent death indexes in these cases.

In other cases, parents could add forenames, or change them, up to 12 months after registration. Sometimes parents forgot to do so, especially prior to 1874, when the onus for registration passed from the registrar to the parents. Additions or alterations to names are entered in the final column of birth certificates, under the heading 'name entered after registration'.

Further Reading
* WOOD, TOM. *An introduction to British civil registration*. 2nd ed. Federation of Family History Societies, 2000.

3. Parish Registers

3A. *Format*
Parish registers of baptisms have been kept since 1538, together with registers of marriages and burials. They continue to be kept even today, and provide an

important alternative source of information on vital events. If you cannot find a particular event in the civil registers, then you should check the parish register.

Until 1813, there was no set format for baptismal entries. Sometimes they were entered chronologically with marriages and burials on the same page. The information given varies. The name of the child, its father, and perhaps its mother, were normally given. Other information, such as the mother's maiden name, the occupation of the father, or the residence of the family, might also be given. During the reign of Mary Tudor, scribes were required to give the names of godparents. This requirement ceased on Elizabeth's accession in 1558, although godparents names can occasionally be found in later registers.

Latin was sometimes used in early registers. This should not pose you a serious problem, since the words used are few, endlessly repeated, and usually have an obvious meaning, for example, *baptizatus*. If you encounter Latin, you may find it useful to consult:

♦ MORRIS, JANET. *A Latin glossary for family and local historians.* Family History Partnership, 2009.

The survival rate of sixteenth-century registers is low. Most of those which do survive are actually copies of the originals, made in accordance with canons of 1597 and 1604. When they were made, the originals were destroyed. Copyists did not, however, necessarily copy everything they saw in the original paper registers. They only recorded what they thought was necessary. Much valuable information was omitted. In particular, the names of godparents, which had been included in parish register entries during Mary's reign, were rarely transcribed.

Survival rates improved in the seventeenth century, although many registers were lost - or never kept - during the tumults of the mid-century, when the task of recording vital events was removed from the clergy and given to lay 'parish registers'. After 1700, most registers survive.

There were two attempts to impose a duty on parish register entries. Both were short-lived, but both left their mark on parish registers. Between 1697 and 1704, and between 1783 and 1794, clergy were required to act as tax collectors. They were very reluctant to do so. Parents were even more reluctant to pay. Some only brought their children for baptism after these duties were repealed; hence a baptism immediately after repeal may be for an older child. Other children were never baptised. Paupers were exempt. This fact is sometime noted in baptismal entries after 1783, where the notation 'P' or 'EP' may denote 'exempt pauper'.

In the late eighteenth century, proposals made by William Dade to improve the information provided in baptism registers were adopted by many clergy, especially in the Dioceses of York and Chester. Dade registers include the father's name, abode, profession, and descent, together with the mother's maiden name and descent. The names of all four grandparents were to be included, as was the date of birth. If you are lucky enough to find your ancestor recorded in a Dade register, you will find much valuable information.

The use of the Dade format was ended by Rose's Act 1812, which set a standard national format for baptismal entries in parish registers. From the beginning of 1813, they had to be made on printed forms which had columns for:

+ When baptised
+ Child's christian name
+ Parents' name (christian and surname)
+ Abode
+ Quality, trade or profession (usually of the father)
+ By whom the ceremony was performed

The reliability of parish registers depends upon the abilities of the scribes who wrote them. Most were reasonably accurate. However, scribes did mis-hear names, and accidentally ran two entries together. In some parishes, registers were written up annually, being copied from small scraps of paper. Mistakes were easily made. Normally, however, the registers will indicate what was written down at the time of a particular event, or at least within twelve months of it. You must use all the sources that you consult with a critical eye, and check that the information you obtain from registers is consistent with the information obtained from other sources.

3B. *Availability*

Parish registers, unless they are still in use, can usually be found in local record offices. Lists of their holdings can frequently be found on their websites, or on A2A **www.nationalarchives.gov.uk/a2a**. Some record offices have published lists in hard copy. More detailed listings, including information about copies and indexes, and covering the holdings of all record offices, can be found in the county volumes of the *National index of parish registers*, published by the Society of Genealogists. These volumes give full details of surviving parish registers, indexes, and copies. They should be consulted by every family historian. Lists are also given in:

+ HUMPHERY-SMITH, CECIL R. *Philimore atlas and index of parish registers*. 3rd ed. Phillimore, 2002.

3C. *Transcripts*

Many transcripts of parish registers have been compiled. In the past, three copies of transcripts were usually made. One was lodged with the relevant local studies library or record office, one with the local family history society, and one deposited with the Society of Genealogists in London. More recently, numerous transcripts and indexes have been compiled as internet databases. These are listed in:

RAYMOND, STUART A. *Births marriages and deaths on the web*. 2nd ed. 2 vols. Federation of Family History Societies, 2005.

The parish pages of Genuki **www.genuki.org.uk** frequently give details of the availability of original parish registers, and sometimes link to web-based transcripts and indexes. A similar service is likely to become available, in time, from Family Search's Research Wiki **https://wiki.familysearch.org/en/Main_Page**, although this is currently in its infancy.

Parish register transcripts have also frequently been published as books or on microfiche/film. Numerous record societies, parish register societies, family history societies, and others, have acted as publishers. Full details of their publications can usually be found on their websites. Most published registers are listed by the Bibliography of British and Irish History **www.history.ac.uk/partners/bbih/faq**. Full listings of published parish registers can be found in the county volumes of my *British genealogical library guides* (formerly *British genealogical bibliographies*). A few printed registers have been digitised for internet websites.

Transcripts and indexes can be very useful if used critically. However, no transcript, and no index, is likely to be 100% perfect - and some leave a great deal to be desired. If a baptismal entry is not found in them, that does not mean that it is not in the original register. It just means that you have to work a little harder to find the entry you require, and check the original register.

Transcripts and indexes should always, if possible, be checked against original registers. This will, of course, be easier, if the latter have been digitised for the internet. At the time of writing, there are only two substantial collections of digitised English parish registers available. The pioneer in this field was Medway Archives **cityark.medway.gov.uk** (click `parish registers online'). This site has recently been joined by Ancestry's 'London Parish Records from 1538' **http://landing.ancestry.co.uk/lma** based on the extensive holdings of London Metropolitan Archives. It is likely that others will follow their lead in the next few years.

It is also possible to consult original parish registers by obtaining microfilms, or having photocopies made. A number of record offices have microfilmed their registers, and made copies available. Consult record office websites for details.

3D. *Indexes*

A wide variety of indexes to births and baptisms are available. The *IGI* (or, to give it its full title, the *International Genealogical Index*), is the single most important index to baptism registers. This is an on-going project run by the Church of Jesus Christ of Latter Day Saints (LDS), popularly known as the Mormons. It is available online at Family Search **www.familysearch.org**. Many libraries hold a fiche version, which was issued in 1992. The *IGI* is also available on CD as the *British vital records index* (2nd ed. 2002). This can be purchased via 'Family Search'. Indexing is still in progress, so it is best to use the website, as it is more up to date. It also provides more information than either the microfiche or the CD. The documents indexed have been microfilmed by the Family History Library in Salt Lake City.

There are two sources for entries in the *IGI*. 'Extracted records' include marriage registers from all denominations, as well as overseas registers. 'Submitted records' have been submitted by researchers tracing their own families, and are frequently very questionable. 'Extracted records' should also be treated with a degree of caution. There will always be errors in indexes. The *IGI* entry gives you a microfilm batch number which can be used to borrow a copy of the document indexed, through the world-wide network of LDS Family History Centres. It is quite likely to provide more information than the index entry, which will only give the names of the child and its parent(s), the date of baptism, and the place. Alternatively (and preferably) you could use the *IGI* information to find the entry in the original register.

Registers filmed and indexed by the *IGI* are listed on Hugh Wallis's '*IGI* Batch Numbers' site **freepages.genealogy.rootsweb.ancestry.com/~hughwallis/IGI BatchNumbers.htm**. 'Genuki' parish pages **www.genuki.org.uk** also frequently provide film numbers of local registers that have been copied.

The documents microfilmed and indexed by the LDS for the *IGI* are not necessarily the original registers. Many bishops transcripts, published registers, and other transcripts, have also been used. Unfortunately, the *IGI* itself does not tell you the status of the document indexed. If you discover an index entry that you need to check, and order the microfilm, you should first determine the status of the document copied. That can only be done by reading the film. The important point to bear in mind is that copies are not as reliable as originals.

Pallot's Baptism Index for England, 1780 - 1837, now held by the Institute of Heraldic & Genealogical Studies **www.ihgs.ac.uk** covers 200,000 baptisms, primarily from London and Middlesex. It was once much more substantial, but much of it was lost in World War II. It is now available on an Ancestry database **www.ancestry.co.uk**. This index is also available on CD.

Family History Online **www.familyhistoryonline.org.uk** formerly had a number of smaller baptism indexes, compiled by family history societies. Most of this data is now available at 'Find My Past' **www.findmypast.org.uk**; however, the original website should be checked for indexes that are now available elsewhere. These can also be found by consulting the websites of individual family history societies, which are listed at **www.genuki.org.uk/Societies.**.

Many of these societies have published baptism indexes on microfiche. Details can be found on their websites. A number of other indexes are listed in Jeremy Gibson & Elizabeth Hampson's *Specialist indexes for family historians*. 2nd ed. Federation of Family History Societies., 2000.

Further Reading

For an up to date guide to parish registers, consult:
- RAYMOND, STUART A. *Parish registers: a history and guide*. Family History Partnership, 2009.

The classic, but now somewhat dated account, is:

♦ STEEL, D.J. *National index of parish registers volume 1. Sources of births, marriages and daeaths before 1837 (1).* Society of Genealogists, 1968.

4. Bishops Transcripts

Bishops' transcripts (sometimes referred to as BTs) are copies of parish registers, made annually, and deposited in diocesan registries. A few survive from the sixteenth century; they continued to be made until the nineteenth century. BTs can now be found in local record offices. They have not survived as well as parish registers, but where the latter have been lost they may be the only record of particular vital events. If parish registers and BTs both survive, it is worth comparing them. BTs sometimes provide additional information.

The county volumes of the *National index of parish registers,* which have already been mentioned, will tell you what survives for particular parishes. For an overall view, consult:

♦ GIBSON, JEREMY. *Bishops transcripts and marriage licences …* 4th ed. Federation of Family History Societies, 1997.

5. Baptismal Certificates

In the late eighteenth- and early nineteenth-centuries, many people needed to prove their age, especially if they wished to enter the civil service or the army. Proof could be had by asking the local clergyman for a baptismal certificate. Unfortunately, their issue was rarely recorded; however, many certificates can be found amongst personnel records. Civil Service evidences of age, which are held by the Society of Genealogists, include many baptismal certificates, and are indexed by Find My Past **www.findmypast.co.uk**. The National Archives (TNA) also holds many certificates for army and naval officers amongst its War Office and Admiralty papers. Full details can be found by using the search box on its website at **www.nationalarchives.gov.uk**

Many baptismal certificates can also be found by consulting A2A **www.nationalachives.gov.uk/A2A**.

6. Non Parochial Registers

Not all Church of England baptisms take place in parish churches. There are also a variety of non-parochial chapels where they may be conducted. Hospitals, workhouses, schools, prisons, and a variety of other institutions all have chapels where baptisms could take place. These institutions frequently have their own baptismal registers, which are listed in the county volumes of the *National index of parish registers.*

The term 'nonparochial registers' is sometimes used to refer to registers kept by nonconformists. It is better to reserve it for institutional records, although it should be noted that a number of important nonparochial registers can be found with nonconformist registers in TNA. There are, for example, some baptisms recorded in the registers of Greenwich and Chelsea Hospitals, in class RG4. Registers from Thomas Coram's Foundling Hospital are also in this class. The Fleet Prison in London was known for the thousands of clandestine marriages that took place there, but its registers also contain baptisms. These are in class RG7. The extensive registers of the British Lying-in Hospital, Holborn, are in class RG8, and include baptisms for the period 1749 to 1868. All of these are now available online, on the BMD Registers site **www.bmdregisters.co.uk**. Unfortunately, this site is one of those which fails to differentiate between nonconformist and nonparochial registers.

7. Nonconformist Registers

'Nonconformist' is the term used in England and Wales for those Protestant Christians who refuse to acknowledge the authority of the Church of England. There are a wide variety of different denominations, but historically the principal ones have been the Presbyterians, Congregationalists (or Independants), Baptists, Methodists, and Quakers. Most nonconformist churches kept registers of baptisms, which generally date from the eighteenth or nineteenth centuries, although some may be earlier. Baptist baptismal registers, of course, record adult baptisms, so may not be of any use to establish dates of birth. Sometimes the Baptists kept birth registers as well.

Nonconformist registers are listed in the county volumes of the *National index of parish registers*. They are also listed in some of the denominational volumes published by the Society of Genealogists in its *My ancestors were* series. These include:

♦ BREED, GEOFFREY. *My ancestors were Baptists: how can I find out more about them?* 4th ed. Society of Genealogists Enterprises, 2007.

♦ CLIFFORD, DAVID J.H. *My ancestors were Congregationalists in England and ales: how can I find out more about them?* 2nd ed. Society of Genealogists, 1997.

♦ LEARY, WILLIAM. *My ancestors were Methodists: how can I find out more about them?* 4th ed. Society of Genealogists Enterprises, 2005.

♦ RUSTON, ALAN. *My ancestors were English Presbyterians or Unitarians: how can I find out more about them?* 2nd ed. Society of Genealogists Enterprises, 2001.

♦ MILLIGAN, EDWARD H., & Thomas, Malcolm J. *My ancestors were Quakers: how can I find out more about them?* 2nd ed. Society of Genealogists, 1999.

After civil registration was introduced in 1837, many nonconformist and other registers were deposited with the Registrar General. These are now held by TNA. A full list of holdings in the two major classes (other than Quaker registers - see below) can be consulted in:

♦ *General Register Office: Registers of births, marriages and deaths surrendered to the Non-parochial Registers Commissions, RG4 & RG8.* 2 vols. List and Index Society, **265-6.** 1996.

Microfilm copies of these registers are often held by local studies libraries and record offices. They are also available online on the BMD Registers site **www.bmdregisters.co.uk.**

The nonconformist registers on this site come from a number of separate TNA classes. These include:

RG4. This is the main series of nonconformist registers, which also includes some non-parochial registers as noted above.

RG5. This class holds two important national registries. The Protestant Dissenters Registry aimed to register the births of dissenters - primarily Presbyterians, Congregationalists and Baptists, although it could be used by anyone. The Registry was established in 1742, but does include retrospective entries dating back to 1716. The Wesleyan Metropolitan Registry fulfilled the same function for Methodists; it was established in 1818.

RG6. The registers of the Society of Friends (Quakers) are held here. These include registers of births, as Quakers did not practise baptism. A full listing is given in:

♦ *General Register Office: Society of Friends registers notes and certificates of births, marriages and deaths (RG 6).* List and Index Society **267**. 1996.

RG8. Not all nonconformist registers were deposited at the end of the 1830s. In 1857, the Non-Parochial Registers Commission tried to collect those which had not so far been deposited. The registers in this class are those they succeeded in collecting.

Most denominations were happy to deposit their registers. The Quakers, however, wanted to keep a record of their own, and created digests of their birth marriage and death registers. These were made in duplicate. One copy was kept by the Monthly Meeting, and may now be in a local record office. The other copy is held by the Library of the Religious Society of Friends. The latter copy has been microfilmed, and is available in major research libraries as:

♦ *Quaker digest registers of births, marriages and burials for England and Wales, c.1650-1837.* 32 reels + pamphlet. World Microfilms Publications, 1989. These digests record some 260,000 births.

8. Huguenot Registers

The Huguenots were French protestants who fled from persecution in the late sixteenth and seventeenth centuries. Many became refugees in England, and established their own churches.

Huguenot registers were deposited with the Registrar General along with nonconformist registers after the introduction of civil registration; these are now in TNA, class RG4. Digitised images of them can be consulted at **www.bmd registers.co.uk**. All of these registers have also been transcribed and published by the Huguenot Society of Great Britain and Ireland **www.huguenot society.org.uk**. The Society's publications are widely available in reference libraries, and are also available for purchase.

9. Roman Catholic Registers

The English church was originally the Roman Catholic church, and parish registers for the reign of Queen Mary (1553-8) were Roman Catholic registers. After her death, Roman Catholics became a persecuted minority, and rarely kept registers until the eighteenth century. A few were deposited with the Registrar General in 1841, and are now in TNA, class RG4. Digitised copies of these can be seen at **www.bmdregisters.co.uk**. Most, however, were retained by the clergy, and not deposited. The majority are now in county record offices, and can be identified in the county volumes of the *National index of parish registers*. A full listing of Roman Catholic registers is provided by:

♦ GANDY, M. *Catholic missions and registers*. 6 vols + index vol. Michael Gandy, 1993.

See also:

♦ STEEL, D.J., & Samuel, Edgar R. *Sources for Roman Catholic and Jewish genealogy and family history*. National index of parish registers **3**. Phillimore for the Society of Genealogists, 1974.

10. Overseas Registers

Births and baptisms which took place overseas could be recorded in a variety of different registers, and must be sought in a variety of locations. Many overseas births and baptisms would have been entered in the registers of foreign jurisdictions. These are beyond the scope of this book, although it is worth pointing out that much information about overseas registration is available on the internet, and can be accessed through the births and baptisms page on Cyndis List **www.cyndislist.com/births.htm**. The Society of Genealogists holds copies of a number of foreign registers. The Family Search site has many 'research helps' on birth and baptism records overseas. It also has the *IGI* (see above, pp.xxx), which indexes many overseas and colonial registers. Microfilmed copies of the overseas documents indexed by the *IGI* can be obtained through the Family History Centres of the LDS.

The British devoted much effort to registering overseas births and baptisms. Consulates, overseas Anglican churches, and the armed forces all kept registers. Births at sea on British shipping were registered by the Registrar General of Shipping and Seamen. Most overseas registers compiled under British jurisdictions are now held in various London repositories.

The Bishop of London was responsible for overseas Anglican churches, and received from them many registers. He also received many baptismal certificates, which were transcribed into registers known as the 'International Memoranda', and which record baptisms conducted at overseas embassies, *etc.*, between 1816 and 1924. These records are now mostly held by Guildhall Library, although a few are in TNA class RG 33 (see below). Details of Guildhall holdings, together with useful notes on registers held overseas, are given on their webpage:

♦ Births, Marriages & Deaths Overseas
   www.history.ac.uk/gh/overseas.htm

A few overseas Anglican registers are also held by:
 • Lambeth Palace Library
   www.lambethpalacelibrary.org/files/Family_History.pdf

The GRO holds registers of births and baptisms compiled by overseas consuls since 1849, and also by the armed forces. Overseas entries in regimental records date back to 1761. The Marine Registers record births on board British merchant and naval vessels since 1837. There are also registers of births on civil aircraft from 1948. For a detailed list of overseas registers in the GRO, see:
 • General Register Events: Overseas Events Orders
   www.gro.gov.uk/gro/content/certificates/faqs-overseas.asp

From 1854, ships captains had responsibility for making returns of births which took place on board their vessels. These were sent to the Registrar General of Shipping and Seamen (RGSS), who compiled registers which are now in TNA:
   1854-87   BT 158
   1875-91   BT 160
   1891-1960 BT 334

The registers for 1854-87 have been digitised at Find My Past **www.findmypast.com**. Births registered by the RGSS should have been reported to the GRO, or, where appropriate, to its Scottish and Irish counterparts. It is not clear that this always happened. If it did, then certificates can be obtained as outlined above, section 2 (or sections 13 and 15 for records from Ireland and Scotland). However, if possible, it is better to consult the original RGSS registers, which are likely to be more accurate than those compiled by the GRO.
More information on records of births at sea can be found in a National Archives research guide:
 • Births, Marriages and Deaths at Sea
   www.nationalarchives.gov.uk/catalogue/RdLeaflet.asp?sLeafletID=246

A number of GRO collections relating to overseas births and baptisms are now held in TNA. Many certificates issued by foreign jurisdictions, copies of register entries made by English overseas clergy, and similar documents, can be found in RG 32. A number of original registers of overseas churches, together with a miscellany of extracts from ecclesiastical and consulate registers *etc* are in RG 33. RG 35 includes notifications to the GRO of births registered in British protectorates in Africa and Asia. All of these classes are indexed in RG 43.
TNA also holds a small number of regimental registers amongst its War Office (WO) collections. These are listed in:
 • BEVAN, AMANDA. *Tracing your ancestors in the National Archives: the website and beyond*. 7th ed. The National Archives, 2006. This volume also has much useful information on overseas births.

In India, chaplains of the East India Company kept registers of baptisms, and sent copies to their London head office. Entries generally relate to people of British descent. Very few relate to Indians. These copies are now held in the British Library's Oriental collections, and have been indexed. For details of these registers, together with information on the Library's search service, consult the 'Ecclesiastical Records' page at

+ India Office Records: Family History Sources
   **www.bl.uk/reshelp/findhelpsubject/history/genealogy/
   indiaofficerecordsfamilyhistory/familyresearch.html**

Further Reading
Only a very brief summary of the resources available for tracing overseas births and baptisms can be given here. Much more detail is provided in the following two books:

+ *The British Overseas: a guide to records of their births, baptisms, marriages, deaths and burials available in the United Kingdom.* 3rd ed. Guildhall Library, 1994.
+ WATTS, CHRISTOPHER T., & Watts, Michael J. *Tracing births, deaths and marriages at sea.* Society of Genealogists Enterprises, 2004.

11. Adopted Childrens Register
The Adopted Childrens Register is a record of all adoptions which have taken place since 1927. This register is not open to public inspection. Adoptees can apply for their own birth certificates, although they may have to attend an interview first. Visit:

+ Adopted Childrens Register
   www.gro.gov.uk/gro/content/adoptions/adoptedchildrenregister/index.asp

12. Channel Islands
The Channel Islands have their own systems of civil registration. Registration of births began on Guernsey in 1840, on Jersey in 1842, on Alderney in 1850, and on Sark in 1925. The Guernsey registers are open to public inspection, and a copy for 1840-1907 is available at the Society of Genealogists (who also hold indexes to 1966). Jersey registers cannot be inspected; the Registrar will search the index and supply certificates for a fee. Some indexes are also held by other institutions, as noted below.

Many parish registers are still with incumbents, although some have been deposited. A full list, with locations, is given in:

+ WEBB, CLIFF. *National index of parish registers ... Channel Islands and the Isle of Man.* Society of Genealogists, 2000.

The Channel Islands Family History Society **www.channelislandshistory.com** has transcribed and indexed most Jersey parish registers. It also holds indexes to the Jersey civil registers up to 1900.

Most Guernsey parish registers are still with incumbents, but many microfilms have been made, and are held by the Priaulx Library. The library also holds copies of the Guernsey civil registers 1840-2004, with indexes. Visit:
+ Priaulx Library
  www.priaulxlibrary.co.uk/priaulx-library-collections-genealogy.asp

Many original parish registers for Jersey, together with indexes to the civil registers up to 1900, are held by:
+ Société Jersiaise
  www.societe-jersiaise.org/library

13. Ireland

13A. *Civil Registers*
The administration of civil registration in Ireland is similar to its administration in England and Wales. Births have been registered since 1864. Since 1st January 1922, vital events in Northern Ireland have been registered separately.

The websites of the two General Register Offices (which include lists of district registrars) are as follows:
+ General Register Office [Eire]
  www.groireland.ie
+ General Register Office (Northern Ireland)
  www.groni.gov.uk

District registrars are also listed by
+ Superintendent Registrars Districts by County
  www.rootsweb.ancestry.com/~bifhsusa/irishregnc.html

The information given in Irish civil birth registers includes date and place of birth, child's forename/s, fathers name, address and occupation, mothers name, and the name and address of the person who registered the birth. From 1903, they include the mother's maiden surname.

The civil registers themselves are not open to direct public access (except through the LDS - see below). Indexes, however, are available. Until 1877, they were compiled annually; thereafter they were quarterly, until 1903, when they again became annual. From 1902, mothers' maiden surnames are given in the indexes. The actual date of birth is recorded from 1864 until 1921.

The indexes provide the basic information needed to order certificates, that is, the name, the Registration District, and the volume and page number in which the entry is recorded. They can be consulted in both Dublin and Belfast offices, but are not available on the internet (although they have been computerized). The Eire office will either provide a birth certificate, or photocopy the entry in the register. The photocopy is cheaper, and is all that is needed for genealogical purposes. The Northern Ireland office will only provide a certificate.

Information from the civil registers is also obtainable from a number of other organizations. Copies of civil registration indexes up to 1958 (1959 for Northern Ireland) are held by the LDS Family History Library, and can be searched online at **http://pilot.familysearch.org/recordsearch/start.html#start.** They are also available on microfilm through its network of Family History Centres. Microfilm copies of the actual registers for some years are also held. These cover births from 1864 to March 1881, and from 1900 to 1913 for the whole of Ireland, births from 1930 to 1955 for Eire, and births from 1922 to 1959 for Northern Ireland. Some of these are searchable on the *IGI*. For details, consult:

+ Family Search Research Wiki: Ireland Civil Registration
  https://wiki.familysearch.org/en/Ireland_Civil_Registration-_Vital_Records

Civil registration indexes are sometimes held by Irish Family History Foundation (IFHF) centres **www.irish-roots.ie**. These usually index the registers held by district registrars, rather than those held centrally. These are the original registers, from which the central registers were copied. They will therefore not reflect any errors made in copying. Consequently, IFHF indexes are likely to produce more accurate information than the Irish GRO indexes. You will, however, need to know the place of your ancestor's birth in order to consult them.

The two Irish GROs also hold a variety of registers recording Irish births overseas. In Dublin, these include consular returns and births at sea from 1864, and armed services registers from 1883. The Belfast office has consular returns and marine registers from 1922, and armed services registers from 1927. Indexes to births at sea are found at the back of each birth index volume until 1921.

More information on civil registration is provided by a number of webpages:

+ From Ireland Genealogy & Family History: Civil Registration in Ireland: Explanation
  www.from-ireland.net/gene/civilregistration.htm
+ Civil Registration
  freepages.genealogy.rootsweb.ancestry.com/
                            ~irishancestors/Civil%20registration.html
+ A Guide to the General Register Office of Ireland
  homepage.eircom.net/%257Eseanjmurphy/gro

13B. *Church Registers*

Irish ecclesiastical registers of baptisms are also available. There are, however, three major differences from English registers. Firstly, more than half of the registers of the Church of Ireland were destroyed by fire in 1922, together with most bishops' transcripts. Secondly, the Church of Ireland, although it was the established church, was not the dominant church. Most Irish were Roman Catholics. There were also many Presbyterians (especially in Northern Ireland), and a number of other denominations. Researchers should note that Roman Catholic and Church of Ireland parishes do not necessarily have the same boundaries or the same names. Thirdly, few registers of any denomination pre-date the late eighteenth century. Irish politics have seldom been conducive to good record keeping.

There was no set form of entry for the baptismal registers of any denomination. Registers of the Church of Ireland are likely to record the child's name and the father's full name, as well as the mother's maiden name. These were the only registers recognised by law, so they sometimes include baptisms of children from other denominations. Recording baptisms in due legal form was important for inheritance purposes.

The baptismal registers of other denominations vary in the information they provide, depending on the whims of scribes. The information may be minimal, or it may be extensive. The names of the child and of its father are normal. Other information may include the mother's name, the father's occupation, the place of residence, etc. Roman Catholic registers are likely to include the names of god-parents.

Many registers of all denominations have been microfilmed for the LDS Family History Library, and indexed in the *IGI* (see above, p.11-12). The National Archives of Ireland **www.nationalarchives.ie/genealogy/church.html** hold some original registers, plus microfilm of others. The Public Record of Northern Ireland **www.proni.gov.uk/index/family_history/family_history_key_sources.htm** also holds many microfilms of registers from all denominations.

For a full listing of Church of Ireland registers, consult:

* REID, NOEL. *A Table of Church of Ireland parochial records and copies.* Irish Family History Society, 1994.

Most registers from the Irish Republic are now deposited in the
* Representative Church Body Library
   www.ireland.anglican.org/genealogy

These are listed in:
* REFAUSSÉ, RAYMOND. *A Handlist of Church of Ireland parish registers in the Representative Church Body Library.* The Library, 2003.
   The Library has published a number of the registers it holds.

Roman Catholic registers are mostly still in the custody of local churches. However, almost all pre-1880 registers (including those from Northern Ireland) have been microfilmed by the National Library of Ireland. For a list, see:

* National Library of Ireland: Parish Registers
   www.nli.ie/en/parish-register.aspx

A comprehensive listing of register transcripts and indexes *etc* is provided by:
* Irish Ancestors Roman Catholic records
   www.irishtimes.com/ancestor/browse/counties/rcmaps

Presbyterian registers are mostly still in local custody. Some registers are held by:
* Presbyterian Historical Society of Ireland
  www.presbyterianhistoryireland.com/index.php?id=library

Most Methodist registers are still in church custody. The Public Record Office of Northern Ireland has many microfilms of registers from churches in the Province.

Quaker registers are held in the Dublin Friends Historical Library, and by the Society of Friends Ulster Quarterly Meeting. For details, visit **www.quakers-in-ireland.ie/archive/indexarc.htm**. Many Northern Ireland Quaker registers are available on microfilm at the Public Record Office of Northern Ireland. Another useful webpage is provided by:
* Family Search Research Wiki: Ireland Church Records
  wiki.familysearch.org/en/Ireland_Church_Records

For a comprehensive guide to Irish ecclesiastical registers, see:
* RYAN, JAMES G., ed. *Irish Church Records*. Glenageary, County Dublin, Ireland: Flyleaf Press, 1992.

Numerous webpages are devoted to Irish registers of baptisms. These are listed in:
* RAYMOND, STUART A. *Irish family history on the web: a directory*. 3rd ed. Family History Partnership, 2007.

14. Isle of Man

The Isle of Man operates its own system of civil registration. Compulsory registration of births began in 1878, although there was an earlier voluntary register dating from 1849, originally intended for nonconformists. An online index to the registers is currently being compiled at **http://manxBMD.com**. The original index is available at Douglas Civil Registry Office. A microfilm of the registers to 1900/1901 is held by the Latter Day Saints, and is available through their Family History Centres.

The registers themselves are not open to public access. Certificates must be obtained from the Registrar. These record the child's forenames, date and place of birth, the father's name and occupation, the mother's name and maiden name, the name of the person reporting the birth, and the date of registration.

The earliest parish registers on the Isle of Man date from 1598. Most are still with incumbents. However, transcripts of all registers were made in 1910, and deposited in the Manx Museum, where they can be consulted on microfilm. These are fully indexed by the IGI (above, p.11-12). A detailed listing of Manx registers is provided by:
* WEBB, CLIFF. *National index of parish registers ... Channel Island and the Isle of Man*. Society of Genealogists, 2000.

Another list, with many extracts, can be viewed at:
* A Manx Note Book: Genealogy
  www.isle-of-man.com/manxnotebook/famhist/genealgy/index.htm
For an overview of sources, consult:
* Sources for Family History
  www.gov.im/lib/docs/mnh/heritage/library/publicinformationsheet1.pdf

15. Scotland

15A. *Introduction*
Family history research in Scotland is far easier than it is in Ireland, or, indeed, in England. This is due to one website:
* Scotlands People
  www.scotlandspeople.gov.uk

Scotlands People has databases of both the civil registers and the old parish registers, as well as the census and probate records. It also has Roman Catholic data, but sadly there are no nonconformist databases.

Alternative resources are also available. If you wish, you can make a personal visit to the Scotlands People Centre to conduct your research. For details, see:
* Scotlands People Centre
  www.scotlandspeoplehub.gov.uk

The Centre has computerized indexes to all civil registers, to the old parish registers, and to a variety of overseas registers. If you are not able to visit, then application can be made for certificates direct to:
* General Register Office for Scotland
  www.gro-scotland.gov.uk
This office also holds the Adopted Childrens Register for Scotland from 1930.

The LDS Family History Library has many microfilm of both the civil registers and the old parish registers. These are indexed by the *IGI*, and are listed at:
* Birth Marriage and Death Records in Scotland
  www.ktb.net/~dwills/scotref/13302-bmdtables.htm

A variety of transcripts and indexes of birth and baptism registers are available on the internet. These are listed in:
* RAYMOND, STUART A. *Scottish family history on the web: a directory.* 2nd ed. Federation of Family History Societies, 2005.

Detailed listings of old parish registers, and of registrars, are given in:
* *The Parishes, Registers and Registrars of Scotland.* Scottish Association of Family History Societies, 1993.

15B. *Civil Registers*

Civil registration in Scotland began on 1st January 1855. Birth registers record the child's name, sex, the date, place and time of birth, and the parents' names (including the maiden surname of the mother), the father's occupation, the name of the informant and his or her relationship to the child. Originally, even more information was included. An 1855 birth certificate also gives information on siblings, the ages and birthplaces of both parents, their usual residence and the date and place of their marriage. These details ceased to be entered from 1856, although the date and place of parents' marriage was reinstated from 1861.

Scotlands People has a database of these registers, including both an index, and digitised images of the actual registers. A number of minor registers have also been indexed. At the time of writing, digitisation of these ends in 1908. They include:

- The Air Register (from 1948) records Scottish births on UK registered aircraft anywhere in the world,
- Consular Returns (from 1914) of Scottish births registered by British consuls
- Foreign Returns (1860-1965), registering births overseas reported by parents.
- High Commission Returns (from 1964), recording Scottish children born in certain Commonwealth countries.
- The Marine Register (from 1855) registering Scottish births on British-registered merchant vessels at sea
- Service Returns (from 1881). These are returns of Scottish births to military personnel abroad.

Microfilm copies of Scottish civil register indexes, 1855-1920 are also held by the Society of Genealogists.

15C. *Old Parish Registers*

The old parish registers (OPRs) were compiled by incumbents of the established (Presbyterian) Church of Scotland. A few commence in 1553, but most are much later. There was no set format, and no equivalent to English bishops' transcripts. The information in the old parish registers is very variable, and can be minimal. The name of the child, the date of baptism and/or birth, and the name of the father, will normally be given. The name of the mother is frequently included. Other information that is sometimes given includes the place or parish of residence, the occupation of the father, and the names (and sometimes occupations) of witnesses. Occasionally, as in, for example, Dundee, witnesses' relationship to the child (if any) may be recorded. Normally, entries relate to children baptised by Presbyterian rites; however, some session clerks also recorded baptisms which took place in other denominations.

Unlike parish registers in England, most Scottish OPRs have been deposited with the Scottish Registrar General. Scotlands People **www.scotlandspeople. gov.uk** provides a full index, together with digitised images of the original registers. The General Register Office for Scotland also holds a Register of neglected entries, listing events proved to have occurred in Scotland between 1801 and 1854 which were not entered in the old parish registers.

Many copies af OPRs are held by Scottish regional record offices, which are listed by the Scottish Archive Network's directory **www.scan.org.uk/directory**. The Scottish Genealogical Society **www.scotsgenealogy.com**, and regional family history societies (listed at **www.safhs.org.uk/SAFHS_Members.asp** frequently also hold copies. Free REG has indexed many OPRs. For details of the parishes covered, visit:

- Counties, Places & Parishes included in the FreeREG Project
  www.freereg.org.uk/parishes/index.shtml

A small number of baptism registers, 1843-1860 are held by the National Archives of Scotland **www.nas.gov.uk/doingResearch/NASrecords.asp**. Other post-1855 parish registers may still be with churches, or may have been deposited in regional record offices. These, together with the registers of other denominations, provide a useful alternative to the civil registers. If your search of the civil registers has proved fruitless, they are worth checking. The Scottish Archive Network (SCAN) database **www.scan.org.uk/aboutus/indexonline.htm**, and Archives Hub **www.archiveshub.ac.uk/cgi-bin/deadsearch.cgi**, may help you to trace them.

15D. *Registers of other Denominations*

A variety of other denominations have been active in Scotland. You can find out which ones have been active in your area of interest by consulting the Statistical Accounts of Scotland 1791-1845. These are available online at **edina.ac.uk/stat-acc-scot/**. They are also available in many libraries.

The National Archives of Scotland **www.nas.gov.uk** hold some registers from the Episcopal Church, together with some microfiche. They also hold a few Quaker, Methodist, and Congregationalist registers. Other registers are held locally. Some - but not all - can be identified by consulting:

- Scottish Archive Network: Online Catalogue
  www.scan.org.uk/catalogue

For seccession registers, consult:

- BAPTIE, DIANE. *Records of baptisms, marriages and deaths in the Scottish secession churches, (including lists of members)* Scottish Association of Family History Societies, 2000. Cover title: *Registers of the Secession Churches in Scotland*

Roman Catholics were a persecuted minority until the mid-eighteenth century. Few registers earlier than 1800 survive. Most registers have been deposited with the Scottish Catholic Archives **www.scottishcatholicarchives. org.uk**. These have been digitised and indexed, and are available on Scotlands People **www.scotlandspeople.gov.uk**.

15E. *Further Reading*

The authoritative, but now somewhat outdated, guide to Scottish registers is:
* STEEL, D.J., & STEEL, A.A.E. *Sources for Scottish genealogy and family history.* National index of parish registers **12**. Society of Genealogists, 1970.

16. Other Sources

The genealogical value of registers of birth and baptisms rests in the fact that they provide evidence of the relationship between parents and children, together with dates. A variety of other sources may provide this information incidentally, although not always with dates. These sources cannot be fully discussed here; however, some notes may be helpful.

16A. *The Census*

Since 1801, a census of the population was taken every ten years. Returns made between 1841 and 1911 should list the occupants of every household in the country, together with their ages. From 1851, they show the relationship between the householder and its occupants, together with exact ages. They thus enable you to identify parents and children, and provide invaluable clues for tracing baptism and birth entries in parish and civil registers. Full details of these returns are given in:
* RAYMOND, Stuart A. *The Census, 1801-1911: a guide for the internet era.* Family History Partnership, 2009.

16B. *Newspapers*

A huge amount of information of relevance to family historians is contained in local newspapers. Of particular significance in the present context are the birth announcements which were frequently made in personal advertisements. These usually indicate at least the name of the child, the names of his parents, and the date of birth. Sometimes more information is given.

Newspapers are difficult to use unless they have been indexed. Fortunately, the British Library is currently digitising and indexing the newspapers in its collections. At the time of writing, 2,000,000 pages from 49 newspapers, both local and national, have been fully digitised and indexed in:
* British Newspapers 1800-1900
  http://newspapers.bl.uk/blcs

Despite the current size of this database, only a small proportion of newspapers in the British Library's collection have so far been digitised. For details of the rest of the collection, visit:

- British Library: Newspaper Collections: a Guide to Our Resources
  www.bl.uk/onlinegallery/newspapers.html

A number of newspapers have digitised their own back runs. If your ancestors were prominent people, they may have placed birth announcements in the *Times*. The *Times index* is widely available in libraries, and also online. The online index can sometimes be accessed free through public library websites:

- Times Online
  archive.timesonline.co.uk/tol/archive

For the *Guardian* and the *Observer*, visit:

- *The Guardian / The Observer* Digital Archive
  http://archive.guardian.co.uk

For Scots, the *Scotsman* is also available online:

- *The Scotsman* Digital Archive
  http://archive.scotsman.com

Most local studies libraries have backruns of newspapers covering their own areas. A comprehensive listing of local newspapers, giving locations, and prepared with the family historian in mind, is provided by:

- GIBSON, JEREMY, LANGSTON, BRETT, & SMITH, BRENDA W. *Local newspapers 1750-1920: England and Wales, Channel Islands, Isle of Man: a select location list.* 2nd ed. Federation of Family History Societies, 2002.

16C. *Bastardy and other Poor Law Records*

We all have bastards amongst our ancestors. In the past, this was frequently a source of great shame, since it often meant that the child would have to be supported by the guardians or overseers of the poor. For family historians, however, a bastard ancestor means that there is another potential source of information - the records generated by Poor Law authorities. Prior to 1834, these could include a bastardy examination (of the mother), a warrant for the appearance of the father, a bastardy bond (binding the father to pay maintainance), and a maintainance order. The law changed in 1834, and other records began to be used. Bastardy documents frequently survive amongst parish, poor law, and quarter session records. They are likely to supply at least the names of the fathers of illegitimate children, and probably much more useful information. For a detailed guide to bastardy records, see:

- PALEY, RUTH. *My ancestor was a bastard: a family historian's guide to sources for illegitimacy in England and Wales.* Society of Genealogists Enterprises, 2004.

It may also be useful to consult:

♦ COLE, ANNE. *Poor law documents before 1834.* 2nd ed. Federation of Family History Societies, 2000.

16D. *Manorial Records*

We also all have manorial tenants amongst our (perhaps earlier) ancestors. The descent of tenancies from father to son are recorded in manorial court rolls, although these do not normally give ages. Heirs had to come into court in order to be formally admitted to their holdings; their appearances were recorded. Heirs' names may also be recorded in deeds, and especially in leases for three lives. Tenants who purchased these leases named their heirs in them, sometimes with their ages. These leases may also be recorded in manorial surveys.

Manorial records can be found in many record offices - although not necessarily where you would expect to find them! They can frequently be located on:

♦ A2A: Access to Archives
www.nationalarchives gov.uk.a2a.

Locations are also given in the:

♦ Manorial Documents Register
www.nationalarchives.gov.uk/mdr

For a detailed guide to manorial records, see:

♦ PARK, PETER B. *My ancestors were manorial tenants.* 2nd ed. Society of Genealogists Enterprises, 2005.

16E. *Inquisitions Post Mortem*

If you are searching for a birth that took place before parish registers become available, then it may be worth checking inquisitions post mortem (IPMs). These inquisitions were taken on the death of feudal tenants who held land directly of the crown, and are available in TNA up to 1646. They record (in Latin) the land held, and, crucially, the name and age of the heir. Full details are given in a TNA research guide:

♦ Inquisitions Post Mortem, Henry III - Charles I : Landholders and Their Heirs
www.nationalarchives.gov.uk/catalogue/researchguidesindex.asp

Many IPMs have been calendared in English. See:

♦ *Calendar of inquisitions post mortem and other analagous documents preserved in the Public Record Office.* HMSO, 1904- . To be continued. The 1st series (16 vols) currently covers 1235-1392; the 2nd series (3 vols) covers 1485-1509.

16F. *Educational Records*

School and university registers usually give the names of parents and dates of birth. Many have been published, and can be found in reference libraries. They are listed in:

- JACOBS, P.M. *Registers of the universities, colleges and schools of Great Britain and Ireland: a list*. Athlone Press, 1966.

A fairly comprehensive collection is held by the Society of Genealogists, whose holdings are listed in:
- *School, university and college registers held in the library of the Society of Genealogists*. 2nd ed. The Society, 1996.

Many unpublished registers can be found in record offices. The registers of nineteenth century elementary schools frequently give birth details, including the names of both parents and siblings. These registers are briefly described, together with other educational records, in:
- CHAPMAN, COLIN R. *Basic facts about using education records*. Federation of Family History Societies, 1999.

16G. *Wills*
Most wills include bequests to all the surviving children of testators. They therefore provide clues for tracing the births and/or baptisms of those children.

Until 1858, wills were normally proved in ecclesiastical courts. The archives of those courts are mostly held in local record offices, although many wills can also be found in TNA. The locations of probate court archives are listed in:
- GIBSON, JEREMY, & CHURCHILL ELSE. *Probate jurisdictions: where to look for wills*. 5th ed. Federation of Family History Societies, 2002.

For a detailed guide to probate records, consult:
- GRANNUM, KAREN, & TAYLOR, NIGEL. *Wills and probate records: a guide for family historians*. 2nd ed. National Archives, 2009.

17. Research Techniques
Tracing family history is not just a matter of pressing a few buttons on the internet. You will also need to tap the memories of your elderly relatives, and to visit record offices and libraries. The latter hold a very wide range of sources, many of which are unlikely ever to make it onto the internet, but which are likely to provide you with vital evidence of your family history. All of the major sources directly relating to birth and baptism information have been discussed here, but there are many other sources of lesser importance which may provide you with vital clues. You need to make yourself aware of them,

You also need to assess the value of the evidence you find. You must ask questions about that evidence. Is it accurate? Does it relate to the family that is being researched? How and why did this particular document come into existence? What was the scribe's intention when he wrote down this information? The vast majority of genealogical sources were not created for genealogical purposes.

There are many pitfalls which the researcher needs to be aware of. It is a myth, for example, that names have always had consistent spellings. They have not, and there are frequently a multiplicity of ways in which to spell a particular name - or, if you prefer, to mis-spell it. Hockey, for example, may be Hokey or Hookey. It is also a myth that, if something is written down, or printed, it is accurate.

Pitfalls are also provided by the very ease with which it is possible to find evidence on the internet. Commercial database providers tend to promise you 'instant' results, and seek custom by presenting you with a search box which will 'enable' you to find your ancestor. They rarely preface their advertising with information about what it is that you are actually searching. But if you do not know the sources of the data they provide, and its evidential value, then the results you obtain are likely to be dubious.

It is for these reasons that family historians need an understanding of the sources their research depends upon. A basic overall introduction by the present author is provided by:

+ RAYMOND, STUART A. *Introducing family history.* Federation of Family History Societies, 2006.

For a guide specifically devoted to the problems involved in using the internet, see:

+ RAYMOND, STUART A. *Netting your ancestors: tracing family history on the interent.* Family History Partnership, 2007.

The most comprehensive guide to family history currently available is:

+ HERBER, MARK. *Ancestral trails: the complete guide to British genealogy and family history.* 2nd ed. Sutton Publishing, 2004.

18. Useful Addresses

18A. *General Register Offices*

Channel Islands

Alderney: The Greffier, Registry for Births, Deaths, Companies, Land and Marriages, St Anne, Alderney, GY9 3AA

Guernsey: H.M. Greffier, The Royal Court House, St Peter Port, Guernsey, GY1 2PB

Jersey: R.J. Kerley, The Superintendent Registrar, 10 Royal Square, St. Helier, Jersey, JE2 4WA **Sark**: The Greffe, La Chasse Marette, Sark, GY9 0SF

England

General Register Office, PO Box 2 , Southport, PR8 2JD

Ireland

General Register Office, Government Offices, Convent Road, Roscommon, Eire

Isle of Man

Douglas Civil Registry Office, Deemsters Walk, Douglas, Isle of Man, IM1 3AR

Northern Ireland
The General Register Office, Oxford House, 49-55 Chichester Street, Belfast,
   BT1 4HL

Scotland
The General Register Office for Scotland, New Register House, 3 West Register
   Street, Edinburgh, Scotland, EH1 3YT

18B. *Other Institutions: England*
Guildhall Library, Aldermanbury, London, EC2V 7HH.
Institute of Heraldic & Genealogical Studies, 79-82 Northgate, Canterbury, Kent,
   CT1 1BA.
Society of Genealogists, 14 Charterhouse Buildings, Goswell Road, London,
   EC1M 7BA.
The National Archives, Kew, Richmond, Surrey, TW9 4DU.
The Library, Religious Society of Friends, Friends House, 173 - 177 Euston Road,
   London, NW1 2BJ.

18C. *Other Institutions: Ireland*
The National Archives, Bishop Street, Dublin 8, Ireland.
Public Record Office of Northern Ireland, 66 Balmoral Avenue, Belfast,
   BT9 6NY This office is due to move in 2010-11. Check **www.proni.gov.uk**
   for their new address.

18D. **Other Institutions:** *Scotland*
The National Archives of Scotland, H M General Register House, 2 Princes
   Street, Edinburgh, EH1 3YY
The Scottish Genealogy Society, 15 Victoria Terrace, Edinburgh, EH1 2JL,
   Scotlands People Centre, HM General Register House, 2 Princes Street,
   Edinburgh, EH1 3YY